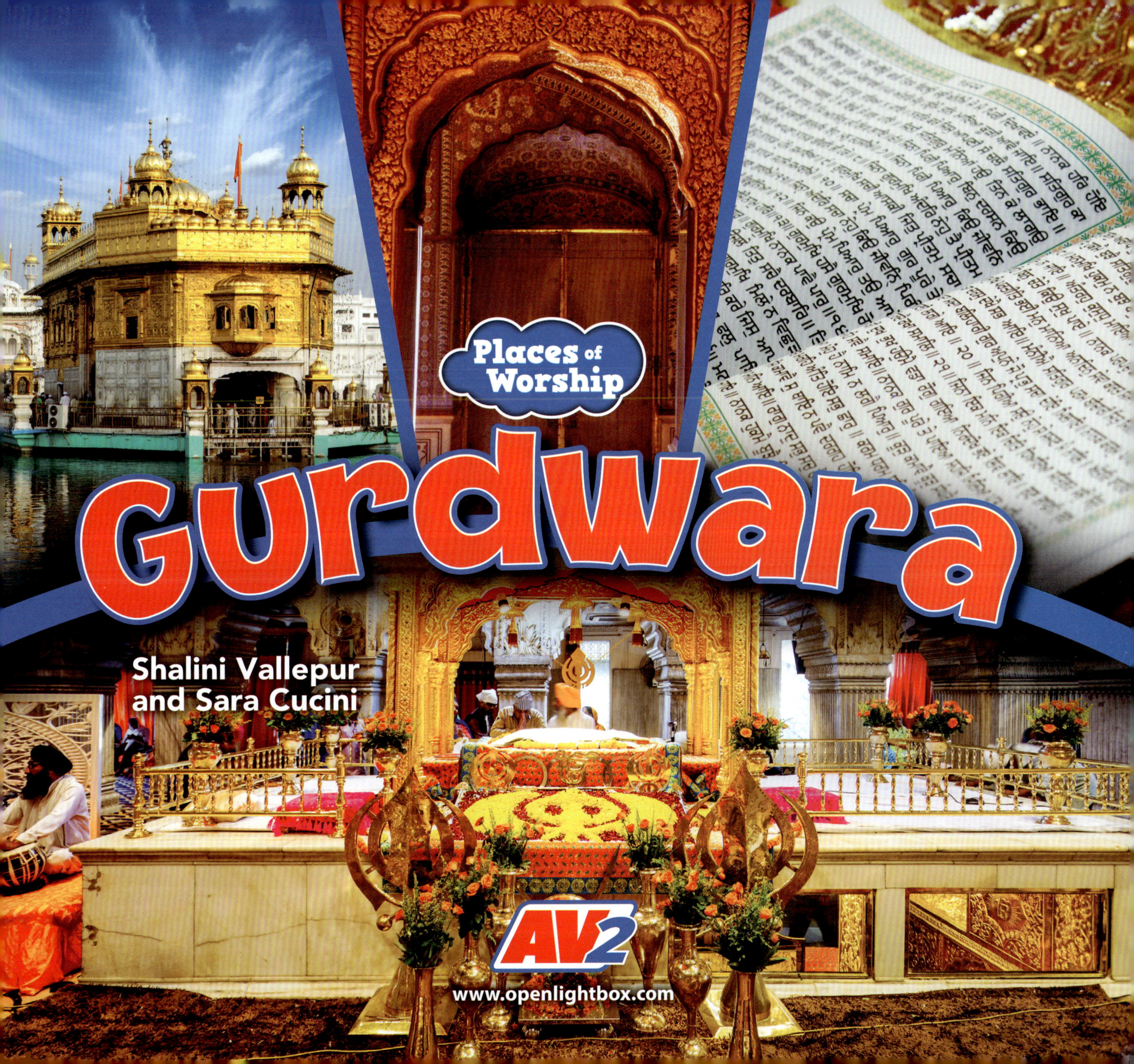
Places of Worship
Gurdwara
Shalini Vallepur
and Sara Cucini
AV2
www.openlightbox.com

Step 1
Go to **www.openlightbox.com**

Step 2
Enter this unique code
ECWGJJGWF

Step 3
Explore your interactive eBook!

AV2 is optimized for use on any device

Your interactive eBook comes with...

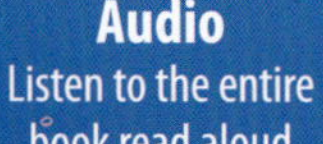

Audio
Listen to the entire book read aloud

Videos
Watch informative video clips

Weblinks
Gain additional information for research

Try This!
Complete activities and hands-on experiments

Key Words
Study vocabulary, and complete a matching word activity

Quizzes
Test your knowledge

Slideshows
View images and captions

Share
Share titles within your Learning Management System (LMS) or Library Circulation System

Citation
Create bibliographical references following APA, CMOS, and MLA styles

This title is part of our AV2 digital subscription

1-Year K–5 Subscription
ISBN 978-1-7911-3320-7

Access hundreds of AV2 titles with our digital subscription.
Sign up for a FREE trial at **www.openlightbox.com/trial**

The digital components of this book are guaranteed to stay active for at least five years from the date of publication.

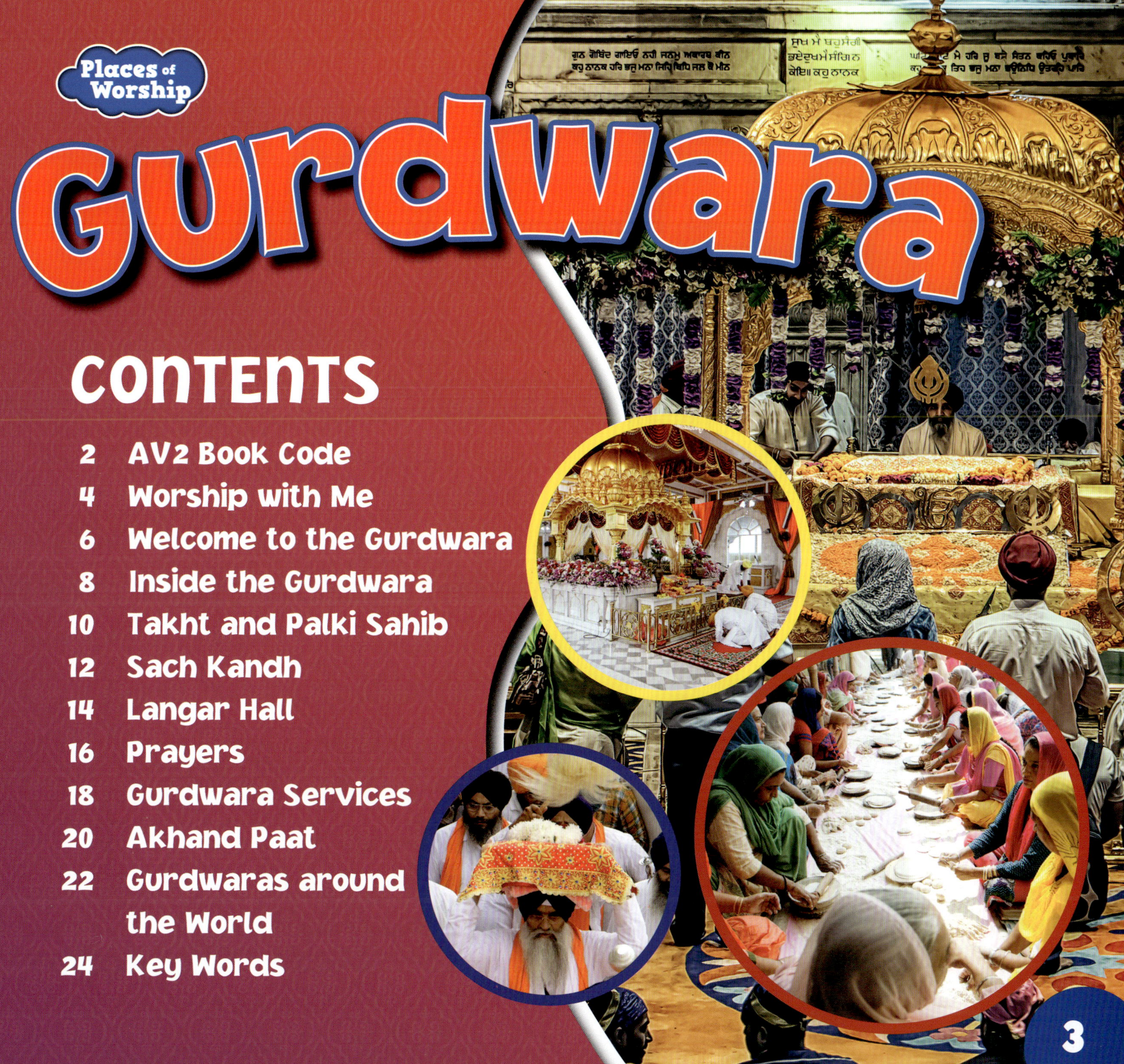

Places of Worship

Gurdwara

CONTENTS

2 AV2 Book Code
4 Worship with Me
6 Welcome to the Gurdwara
8 Inside the Gurdwara
10 Takht and Palki Sahib
12 Sach Kandh
14 Langar Hall
16 Prayers
18 Gurdwara Services
20 Akhand Paat
22 Gurdwaras around the World
24 Key Words

Worship with Me

Have you ever been to a gurdwara? A gurdwara is a place of worship for followers of **Sikhism**, called **Sikhs**.

Sikhism started around the year 1500 AD.

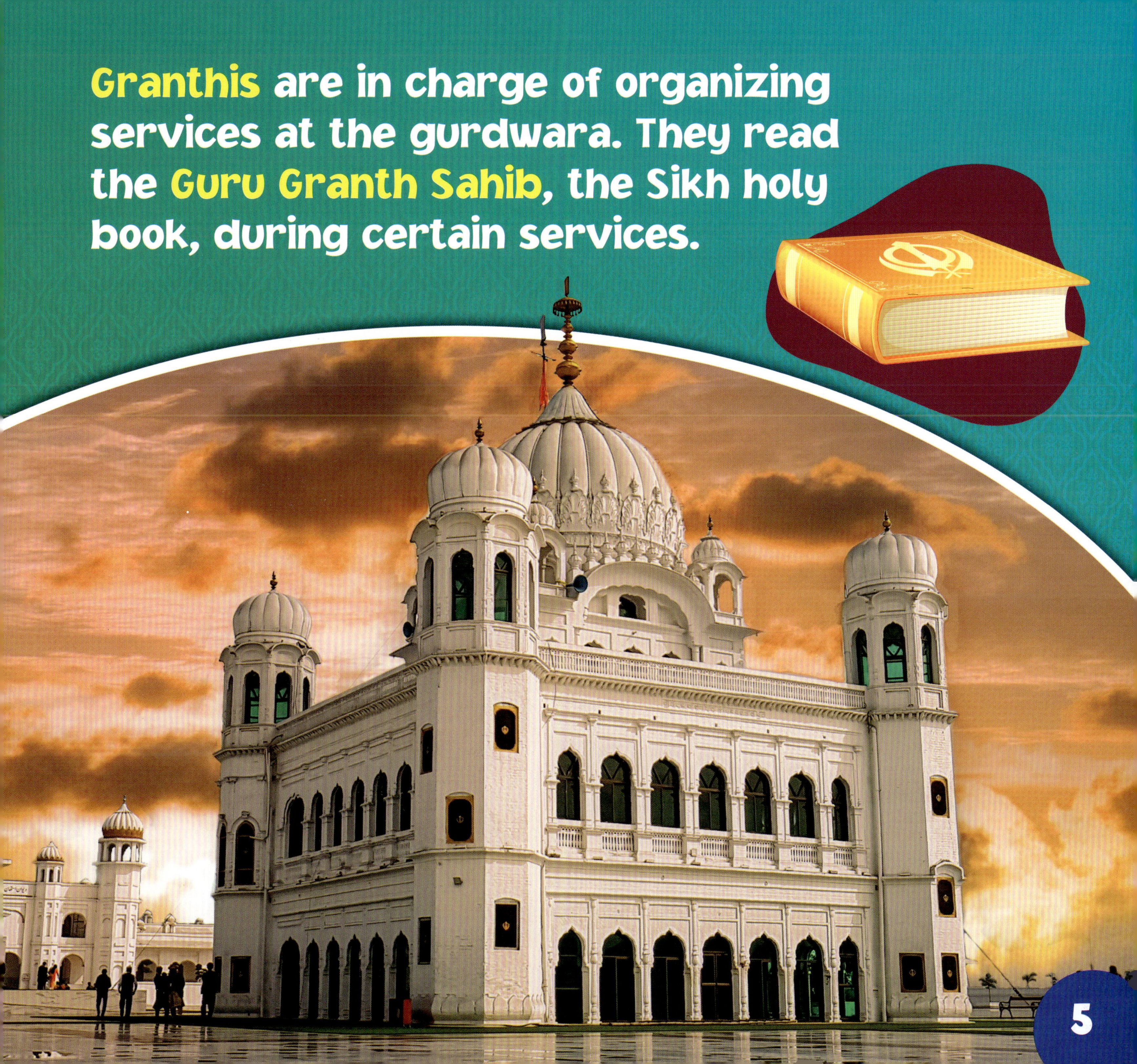

Granthis are in charge of organizing services at the gurdwara. They read the **Guru Granth Sahib**, the Sikh holy book, during certain services.

Welcome to the Gurdwara

There are gurdwaras all over the world. They may look very different from each other.

Most gurdwaras have a domed roof called **gumbad**. Gurwaras often have **more than one entrance**. This shows that **everybody is welcome**, no matter where they come from.

Every gurdwara has a **Nishan Sahib**. This is an orange **flag** with a Sikh symbol on it.

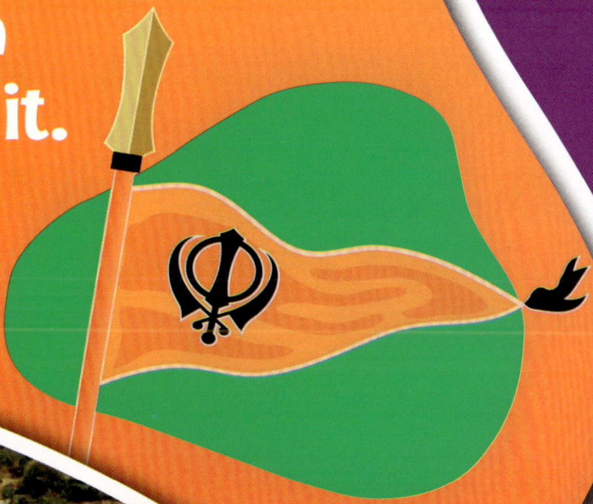

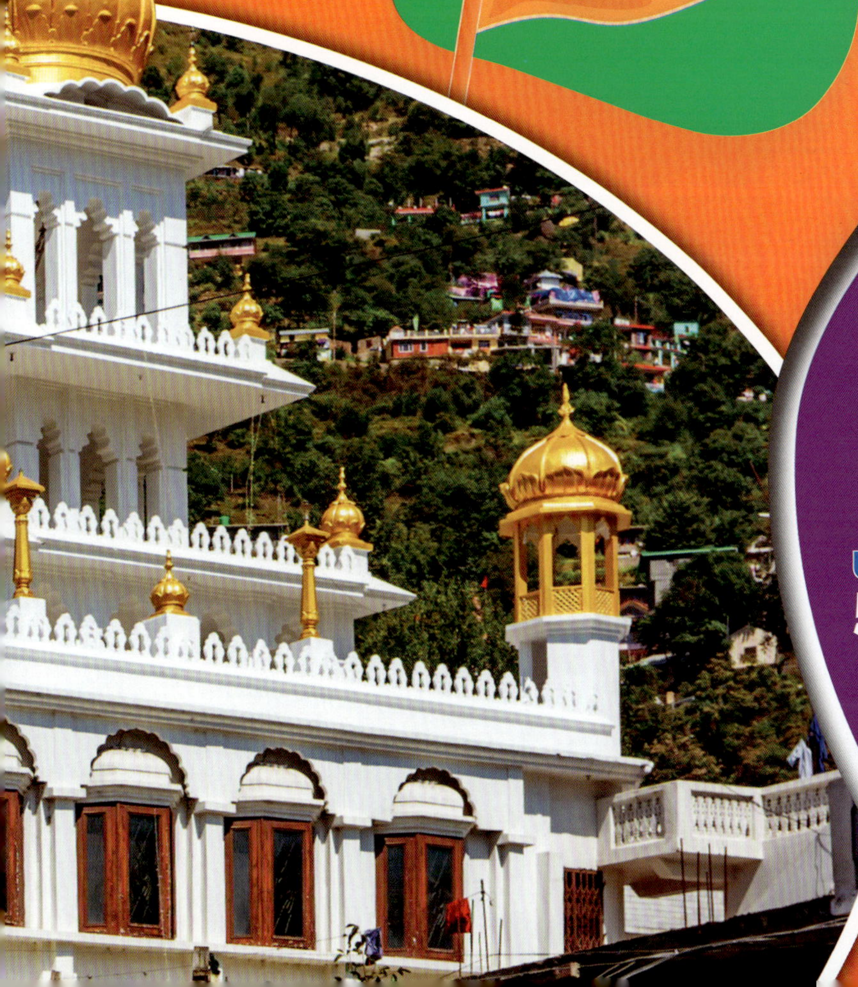

Sikh World Population

About 25 million people around the world identify as Sikh.

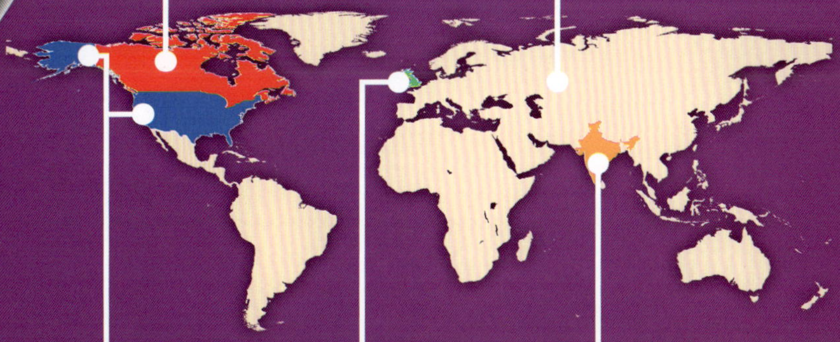

Canada
650,000 Sikhs

Other Countries
1.4 million Sikhs

United States
500,000 Sikhs

India
22 million Sikhs

United Kingdom
450,000 Sikhs

Inside the Gurdwara

People remove their shoes and cover their heads in the gurdwara. Men, boys, and women cover their heads with different kinds of headcovers called **pagri**, **patka**, and **chunni**.

The **Darbar Sahib** is the main area of worship. There are usually no chairs in the Darbar Sahib. Most people sit on the floor during worship.

Takht and Palki Sahib

At the front or middle of the Darbar Sahib is the throne, or **Takht**. This is a raised platform. On top of the Takht is a **canopy**. It is part of a structure called the **Palki Sahib**.

The Guru Granth Sahib is placed on the Takht every morning at dawn. Placing the Guru Granth Sahib on the Takht is called **Prakash**.

Sach Kandh

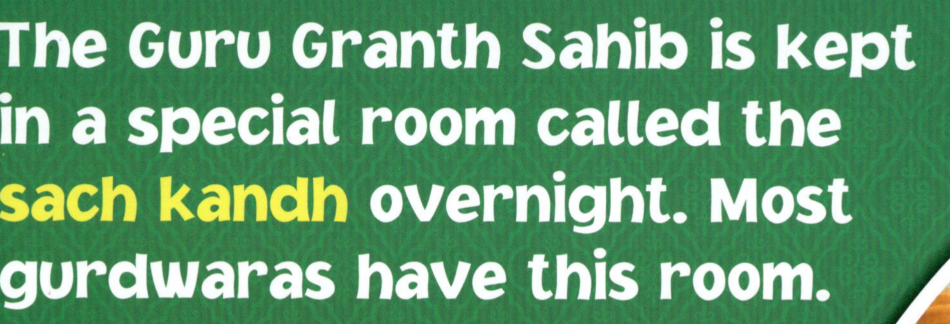

The Guru Granth Sahib is kept in a special room called the **sach kandh** overnight. Most gurdwaras have this room.

Sikhs follow the teachings of **11 Gurus**, or leaders. Of these, 10 were people. The Guru Granth Sahib book is considered the 11th, **final Guru.**

The Guru Granth Sahib is wrapped in a special **cloth** and carried on the head of a Granthi when it is moved to and from the sach kandh.

Langar Hall

Most gurdwaras have a Langar hall. This is a **kitchen** and **eating area**. Food is cooked by volunteers. Anybody in the gurdwara and the community can visit the Langar hall for a free meal.

Vegetarian food is served in the Langar hall. Everybody sits on the floor to eat. Those who can afford to will give a **donation** of money or food and help to serve people.

Prayers

There are different prayers in Sikhism. **Panj Bania** means five daily prayers. The prayers are written in a book called a **Gutka**.

Most gurdwaras stay open all the time, but prayers can take place **anywhere**.

Daily Prayers

Morning Prayers

Three prayers said after sunrise

Evening Prayer

A fourth prayer to be said at sunset

Bedtime Prayer

The fifth and last prayer to be said before going to sleep

Gurdwara Services

Many Sikhs cannot visit the gurdwara every day to pray. In some countries, there is a **longer prayer service** on the **weekend**, when more people are free.

During the service, people sing special songs called **kirtan**. After services or prayer, everybody is given a sweet food called **karah parshad**. It is a gift from the gurdwara and the Gurus.

Akhand Paat

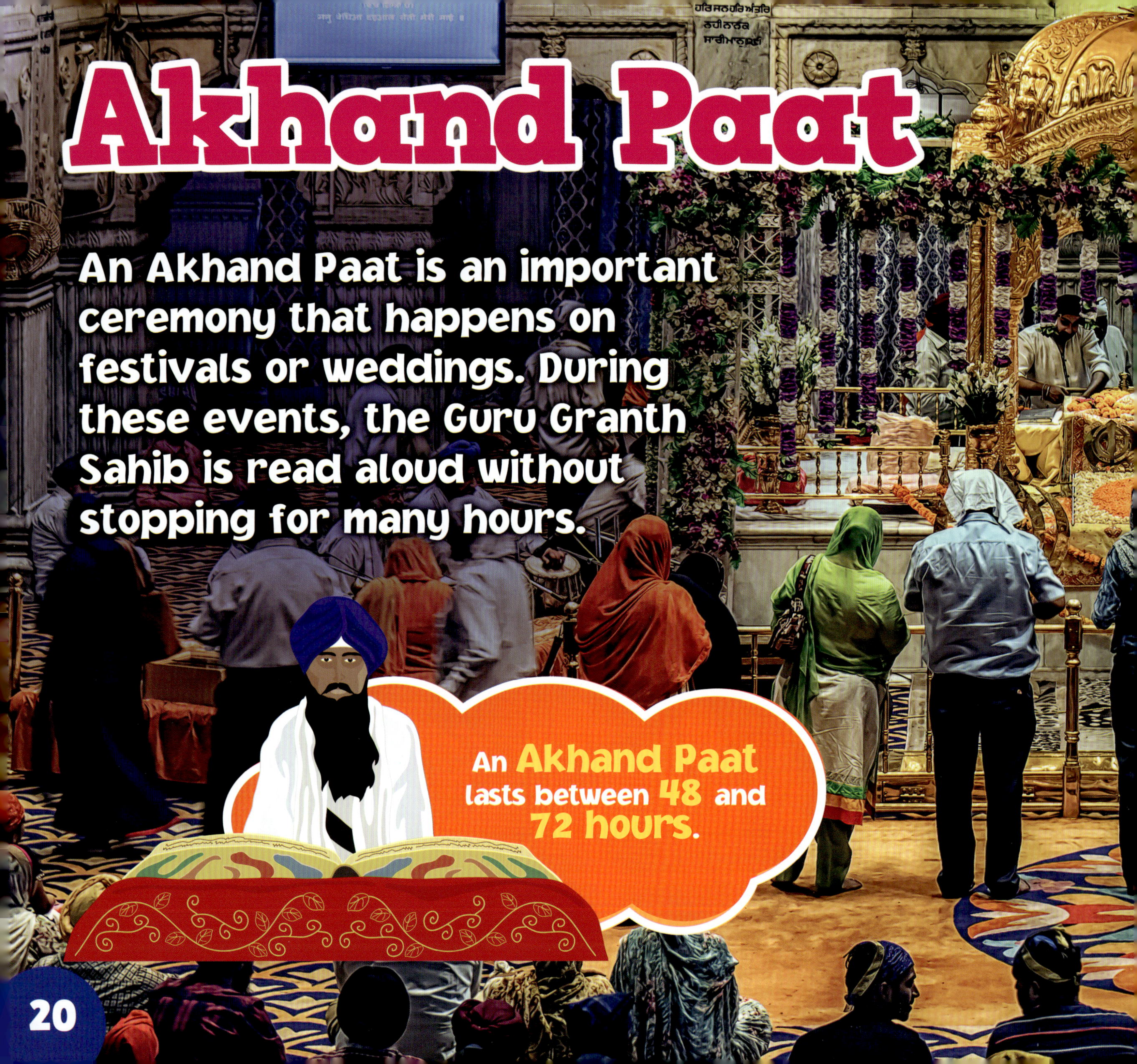

An Akhand Paat is an important ceremony that happens on festivals or weddings. During these events, the Guru Granth Sahib is read aloud without stopping for many hours.

An **Akhand Paat** lasts between **48** and **72 hours.**

The Akhand Paat usually happens at the gurdwara. Everybody comes together to hear the **lessons** from the Guru Granth Sahib.

Gurdwaras around the World

Sri Guru Singh Sabha Southall Gurdwara
London, United Kingdom

Guru Nanak Darbar Dubai Gurdwara
Dubai, United Arab Emirates

Sikh Gurdwara Sahib
San Jose, California, United States

Sri Harimandir Sahib Gurdwara
Amritsar, India

KEY WORDS

Research has shown that as much as 65 percent of all written material published in English is made up of 300 words. These 300 words cannot be taught using pictures or learned by sounding them out. They must be recognized by sight. This book contains 94 common sight words to help young readers improve their reading fluency and comprehension. This book also teaches young readers several important content words, such as proper nouns.

Page	Sight Words First Appearance
4	a, around, been, for, have, is, me, of, place, started, the, to, with, year, you
5	are, at, book, in, read, they
6	all, come, different, each, from, look, may, more, most, no, often, one, other, over, shows, than, that, there, this, very, where, world
7	about, an, as, every, has, it, miles, on, people, states
8	and, boys, heads, kinds, men, their
10	or, part
11	by
12	follow, these, were
13	when
14	can, food
15	eat, give, help, those, who, will
16	but, means, open, take, time
17	after, be, before, last, said, three
18	day, many, some
19	songs
20	between, important, without
21	hear, together

Page	Content Words First Appearance
4	followers, gurdwara, Sikhism, Sikhs, worship
5	Granthis, Guru Granth Sahib, services
6	entrance, gumbad, roof
7	Canada, countries, flag, India, Nishan Sahib, population, symbol, United Kingdom United States
8	chunni, headcovers, pagri, patka, shoes, women
9	area, chairs, Darbar Sahib, floor
10	canopy, Palki Sahib, platform, structure, Takht, throne
11	cloth, dawn, morning, Prakash
12	gurus, leaders, room, sach kandh, teachings
14	community, kitchen, Langar hall, meal, volunteers
15	donation, money
16	Gutka, Panj Banja, prayers
17	sunrise, sunset
18	weekend
19	gift, karah parshad, kirtan
20	Akhand Paat, ceremony, events, festivals, hours, weddings
21	lessons

Published by Lightbox Learning Inc.
276 5th Avenue, Suite 704 #917
New York, NY 10001
Website: www.openlightbox.com

Library of Congress Control Number: 2024935537

ISBN 978-1-5105-8185-2 (hardcover)
ISBN 979-8-8745-1510-2 (softcover)
ISBN 978-1-5105-8186-9 (static multi-user eBook)
ISBN 978-1-5105-8188-3 (interactive multi-user eBook)

Printed in Guangzhou, China
1 2 3 4 5 6 7 8 9 0 28 27 26 25 24

052024
100923

Project Coordinator: Sara Cucini
Designer: Jean Faye Rodriguez

Every reasonable effort has been made to trace ownership and to obtain permission to reprint copyright material. The publisher would be pleased to have any errors or omissions brought to its attention so that they may be corrected in subsequent printings.

The publisher acknowledges Getty Images, Alamy, and Shutterstock as the primary image suppliers for this title.

First published by BookLife in 2020.